This Book Belongs to

_____

_____

_____

Note: if using real makeup, allow page to dry completely before turning or closing. A short burst from a hair dryer can aid this process.

Style _____

Trends _____

_____

Inspiration _____

_____

Textiles _____

_____

Notes _____

_____

Swatches

Details

Name of Look _____

Evening ◯
Daytime ◯

Face

Moisturizer

_____

Concealer

_____

Foundation

_____

Highlight/Blush

_____

Eyes

Brows

_____

Eyelid

_____

Liner

_____

Crease

_____

Mascara

_____

Lips

Liner

_____

Lip Color

_____

Gloss

_____

Notes

Style _____

Trends _____
_____

Inspiration _____
_____

Textiles _____
_____

Notes _____
_____

Swatches

Details

Name of Look _____

Evening ◯
Daytime ◯

Face

Moisturizer

_____

Concealer

_____

Foundation

_____

Highlight/Blush

_____

Eyes

Brows

_____

Eyelid

_____

Liner

_____

Crease

_____

Mascara

_____

Lips

Liner

_____

Lip Color

_____

Gloss

_____

Notes

Style _____

Trends _____

_____

Inspiration _____

_____

Textiles _____

_____

Notes _____

_____

Swatches

Details

Name of Look _____

Evening ◯
Daytime ◯

Face

Moisturizer

_____

Concealer

_____

Foundation

_____

Highlight/Blush

_____

Eyes

Brows

_____

Eyelid

_____

Liner

_____

Crease

_____

Mascara

_____

Lips

Liner

_____

Lip Color

_____

Gloss

_____

Notes

Style _____

Trends _____

_____

Inspiration _____

_____

Textiles _____

_____

Notes _____

_____

Swatches

Details

Name of Look _____

Evening ◯
Daytime ◯

Face

Moisturizer

_____

Concealer

_____

Foundation

_____

Highlight/Blush

_____

Eyes

Brows

_____

Eyelid

_____

Liner

_____

Crease

_____

Mascara

_____

Lips

Liner

_____

Lip Color

_____

Gloss

_____

Notes

Style _____

Trends _____
_____

Inspiration _____
_____

Textiles _____
_____

Notes _____
_____

Swatches

Details

Name of Look _____

Evening ◯
Daytime ◯

Face

Moisturizer
_____

Concealer
_____

Foundation
_____

Highlight/Blush
_____

Eyes

Brows
_____

Eyelid
_____

Liner
_____

Crease
_____

Mascara
_____

Lips

Liner
_____

Lip Color
_____

Gloss
_____

Notes

Style _____

Trends _____

_____

Inspiration _____

_____

Textiles _____

_____

Notes _____

_____

Swatches

Details

Name of Look _____

Evening ◯
Daytime ◯

Face

Moisturizer

_____

Concealer

_____

Foundation

_____

Highlight/Blush

_____

Eyes

Brows

_____

Eyelid

_____

Liner

_____

Crease

_____

Mascara

_____

Lips

Liner

_____

Lip Color

_____

Gloss

_____

Notes

Style _____

Trends _____
_____

Inspiration _____
_____

Textiles _____
_____

Notes _____
_____

Swatches

Details

Name of Look _____

Evening ◯
Daytime ◯

Face

Moisturizer

_____

Concealer

_____

Foundation

_____

Highlight/Blush

_____

Eyes

Brows

_____

Eyelid

_____

Liner

_____

Crease

_____

Mascara

_____

Lips

Liner

_____

Lip Color

_____

Gloss

_____

Notes

Style _____

Trends _____
_____
_____

Inspiration _____
_____

Textiles _____
_____

Notes _____
_____

Swatches

Details

Name of Look _____

Evening ◯
Daytime ◯

Face

Moisturizer
_____

Concealer
_____

Foundation
_____

Highlight/Blush
_____

Eyes

Brows
_____

Eyelid
_____

Liner
_____

Crease
_____

Mascara
_____

Lips

Liner
_____

Lip Color
_____

Gloss
_____

Notes

Style _____

Trends _____
_____
_____

Inspiration _____
_____

Textiles _____
_____

Notes _____
_____

Swatches

Details

Name of Look _____

Evening ◯
Daytime ◯

Face

Moisturizer

_____

Concealer

_____

Foundation

_____

Highlight/Blush

_____

Eyes

Brows

_____

Eyelid

_____

Liner

_____

Crease

_____

Mascara

Lips

Liner

_____

Lip Color

_____

Gloss

_____

Notes

Style _____

Trends _____

_____

_____

Inspiration _____

_____

_____

Textiles _____

_____

_____

Notes _____

_____

Swatches

Details

Name of Look _____

Evening ◯
Daytime ◯

Face

Moisturizer

_____

Concealer

_____

Foundation

_____

Highlight/Blush

_____

Eyes

Brows

_____

Eyelid

_____

Liner

_____

Crease

_____

Mascara

_____

Lips

Liner

_____

Lip Color

_____

Gloss

_____

Notes

Style _____

Trends _____
_____

Inspiration _____
_____

Textiles _____
_____

Notes _____
_____

Swatches

Details

Name of Look _____

Evening ○
Daytime ○

Face
Moisturizer

_____

Concealer

_____

Foundation

_____

Highlight/Blush

_____

Eyes
Brows

_____

Eyelid

_____

Liner

_____

Crease

_____

Mascara

_____

Lips
Liner

_____

Lip Color

_____

Gloss

_____

Notes

Style _____

Trends _____

_____

Inspiration _____

_____

Textiles _____

_____

Notes _____

_____

Swatches

Details

Name of Look _____

Evening ◯
Daytime ◯

Face

Moisturizer

_____

Concealer

_____

Foundation

_____

Highlight/Blush

_____

Eyes

Brows

_____

Eyelid

_____

Liner

_____

Crease

_____

Mascara

_____

Lips

Liner

_____

Lip Color

_____

Gloss

_____

Notes

Style _____

Trends _____

_____

Inspiration _____

_____

Textiles _____

_____

Notes _____

_____

Swatches

Details

Name of Look _____

Evening ◯
Daytime ◯

Face
Moisturizer
_____

Concealer
_____

Foundation
_____

Highlight/Blush
_____

Eyes
Brows
_____

Eyelid
_____

Liner
_____

Crease
_____

Mascara
_____

Lips
Liner
_____

Lip Color
_____

Gloss
_____

Notes

Style _____

Trends _____
_____
_____

Inspiration _____
_____

Textiles _____
_____

Notes _____
_____

Swatches

Details

Name of Look _____

Evening ○
Daytime ○

Face

Moisturizer

_____

Concealer

_____

Foundation

_____

Highlight/Blush

_____

Eyes

Brows

_____

Eyelid

_____

Liner

_____

Crease

_____

Mascara

_____

Lips

Liner

_____

Lip Color

_____

Gloss

_____

Notes

Style _____

Trends _____
_____

Inspiration _____
_____

Textiles _____
_____

Notes _____
_____

Swatches

Details

Name of Look _____

Evening ◯
Daytime ◯

Face

Moisturizer

_____

Concealer

_____

Foundation

_____

Highlight/Blush

_____

Eyes

Brows

_____

Eyelid

_____

Liner

_____

Crease

_____

Mascara

_____

Lips

Liner

_____

Lip Color

_____

Gloss

_____

Notes

Style _____

Trends _____
_____
_____

Inspiration _____
_____
_____

Textiles _____
_____
_____

Notes _____
_____

Swatches

Details

Name of Look _____

Evening ○
Daytime ○

Face

Moisturizer

_____

Concealer

_____

Foundation

_____

Highlight/Blush

_____

Eyes

Brows

_____

Eyelid

_____

Liner

_____

Crease

_____

Mascara

_____

Lips

Liner

_____

Lip Color

_____

Gloss

_____

Notes

Style _____

Trends _____
_____

Inspiration _____
_____

Textiles _____
_____

Notes _____
_____

Swatches

Details

Name of Look _____

Evening ○
Daytime ○

Face
Moisturizer

_____

Concealer

_____

Foundation

_____

Highlight/Blush

_____

Eyes
Brows

_____

Eyelid

_____

Liner

_____

Crease

_____

Mascara

_____

Lips
Liner

_____

Lip Color

_____

Gloss

_____

Notes

Style _____

Trends _____

_____

Inspiration _____

_____

Textiles _____

_____

Notes _____

_____

Swatches

Details

Name of Look _____

Evening ◯
Daytime ◯

Face
Moisturizer

_____

Concealer

_____

Foundation

_____

Highlight/Blush

_____

Eyes

Brows

_____

Eyelid

_____

Liner

_____

Crease

_____

Mascara

_____

Lips

Liner

_____

Lip Color

_____

Gloss

_____

Notes

Style _____

Trends _____
_____
_____

Inspiration _____
_____

Textiles _____
_____

Notes _____
_____

Swatches

Details

Name of Look _____

Evening ○
Daytime ○

Face

Moisturizer

_____

Concealer

_____

Foundation

_____

Highlight/Blush

_____

Eyes

Brows

_____

Eyelid

_____

Liner

_____

Crease

_____

Mascara

_____

Lips

Liner

_____

Lip Color

_____

Gloss

_____

Notes

Style _____

Trends _____
_____

Inspiration _____
_____

Textiles _____
_____

Notes _____
_____

Swatches

Details

Name of Look _____

Evening ◯
Daytime ◯

Face

Moisturizer

_____

Concealer

_____

Foundation

_____

Highlight/Blush

_____

Eyes

Brows

_____

Eyelid

_____

Liner

_____

Crease

_____

Mascara

_____

Lips

Liner

_____

Lip Color

_____

Gloss

_____

Notes

Style _____

Trends _____
_____
_____

Inspiration _____
_____

Textiles _____
_____

Notes _____
_____

Swatches

Details

Name of Look _____

Evening ○
Daytime ○

Face
Moisturizer
_____

Concealer
_____

Foundation
_____

Highlight/Blush
_____

Eyes
Brows
_____

Eyelid
_____

Liner
_____

Crease
_____

Mascara
_____

Lips
Liner
_____

Lip Color
_____

Gloss
_____

Notes

Style _____

Trends _____
_____
_____

Inspiration _____
_____

Textiles _____
_____

Notes _____
_____

Swatches

Details

Name of Look _____

Evening ○
Daytime ○

Face

Moisturizer

_____

Concealer

_____

Foundation

_____

Highlight/Blush

_____

Eyes

Brows

_____

Eyelid

_____

Liner

_____

Crease

_____

Mascara

_____

Lips

Liner

_____

Lip Color

_____

Gloss

_____

Notes

Style _____

Trends _____

_____

Inspiration _____

_____

Textiles _____

_____

Notes _____

_____

Swatches

Details

Name of Look _____

Evening ○
Daytime ○

Face

Moisturizer

_____

Concealer

_____

Foundation

_____

Highlight/Blush

_____

Eyes

Brows

_____

Eyelid

_____

Liner

_____

Crease

_____

Mascara

_____

Lips

Liner

_____

Lip Color

_____

Gloss

_____

Notes

Style _____

Trends _____

_____

Inspiration _____

_____

Textiles _____

_____

Notes _____

_____

Swatches

Details

Name of Look _____

Evening ⭘
Daytime ⭘

Face

Moisturizer

_____

Concealer

_____

Foundation

_____

Highlight/Blush

_____

Eyes

Brows

_____

Eyelid

_____

Liner

_____

Crease

_____

Mascara

_____

Lips

Liner

_____

Lip Color

_____

Gloss

_____

Notes

Style _____

Trends _____
_____
_____

Inspiration _____
_____
_____

Textiles _____
_____
_____

Notes _____
_____

Swatches

Details

Name of Look _____

Evening ○
Daytime ○

Face
Moisturizer

_____

Concealer

_____

Foundation

_____

Highlight/Blush

_____

Eyes
Brows

_____

Eyelid

_____

Liner

_____

Crease

_____

Mascara

_____

Lips
Liner

_____

Lip Color

_____

Gloss

_____

Notes

Style _____

Trends _____

_____

Inspiration _____

_____

Textiles _____

_____

Notes _____

_____

Swatches

Details

Name of Look _____

Evening ○
Daytime ○

Face

Moisturizer

_____

Concealer

_____

Foundation

_____

Highlight/Blush

_____

Eyes

Brows

_____

Eyelid

_____

Liner

_____

Crease

_____

Mascara

_____

Lips

Liner

_____

Lip Color

_____

Gloss

_____

Notes

Style _____

Trends _____
_____
_____

Inspiration _____
_____

Textiles _____
_____

Notes _____
_____

Swatches

Details

Name of Look _____

Evening ○
Daytime ○

Face
Moisturizer

_____

Concealer

_____

Foundation

_____

Highlight/Blush

_____

Eyes
Brows

_____

Eyelid

_____

Liner

_____

Crease

_____

Mascara

_____

Lips
Liner

_____

Lip Color

_____

Gloss

_____

Notes

Made in the USA
Middletown, DE
30 April 2021